THIS BOOK
BELONGS TO:

_____

Let's provide our new generation with the tools they need to grow up with a better understanding of science and technology. *The Technical Alphabet* is a powerful tool to introduce young minds to the technology around them.

STEM Center USA inspires the next generation of STEM (Science Technology Engineering Math) leaders by developing a passion for STEM careers at a young age and maintaining interest throughout middle and high school. We provide students with an experiential education through our robotics creativity centers, school programs, and product line.

www.STEMCenterUSA.com

The Technical Alphabet®
Second Edition, 2015
ISBN 978-0-9960862-2-6

The

TECHNICAL

Technology Literacy
starts with the ABCs

ALPHABET

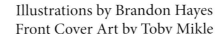

Illustrations by Brandon Hayes
Front Cover Art by Toby Mikle

A

Axle

An **axle** is a rod that a wheel rotates around. You can see **axles** on the bottom of a train.

B

Beam

A **beam** is the basic building block of a structure.
Beams are used to make buildings and bridges.

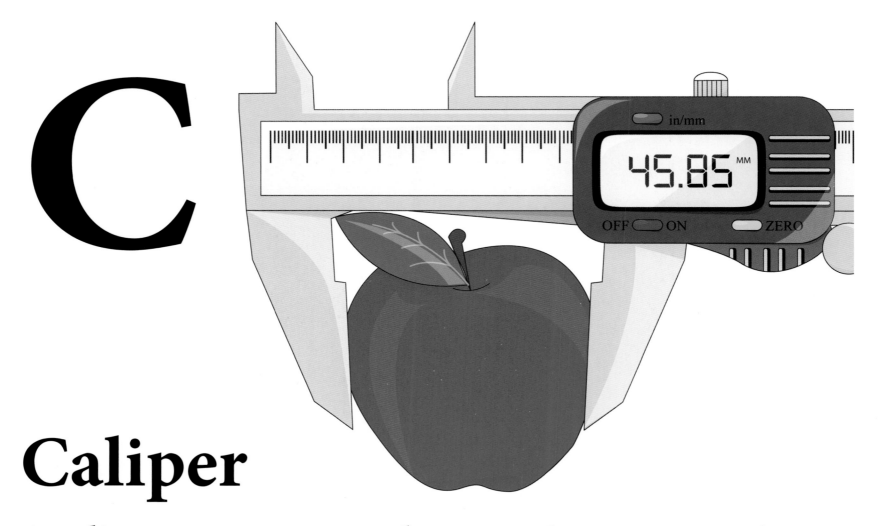

Caliper

A **caliper** is a measuring device. **Calipers** are used to make accurate measurements of small objects.

D

Drill

A **drill** is a rotating tool to make holes. **Drills** can also be used to drive screws.

E

Engine

An **engine** is a machine with moving parts. It makes your car move by converting energy to motion.

L

Lever

A **lever** is a rod that rests on a pivot point. **Levers** make it easy to lift heavy objects like this big rock.

M

Mallet

A **mallet** is a hammer-like tool with a wooden or rubber head. **Mallets** are used on soft surfaces without leaving a mark.

13

N

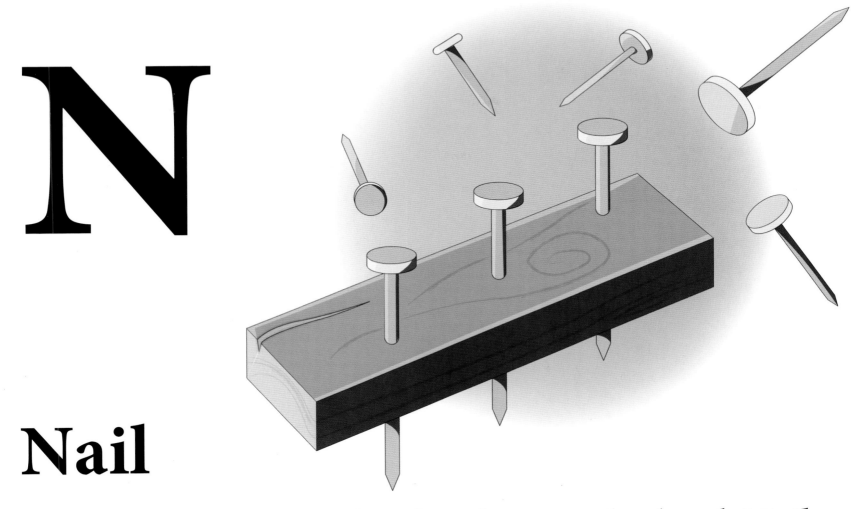

Nail

A **nail** is a sharp, metal rod with a circular head. **Nails** are driven into wood to join them.

O

Oar

An **oar** is a long pole with a broad blade at one end. An **oar** works as a lever to row a boat.

P

Pulley

A **pulley** is a simple machine made of a wheel and a rope. Multiple **pulleys** work together to easily carry heavy things.

Q

Quasar

Quasars exist in galaxies with massive black holes.
Quasars outshine all other stars in their galaxy.

R

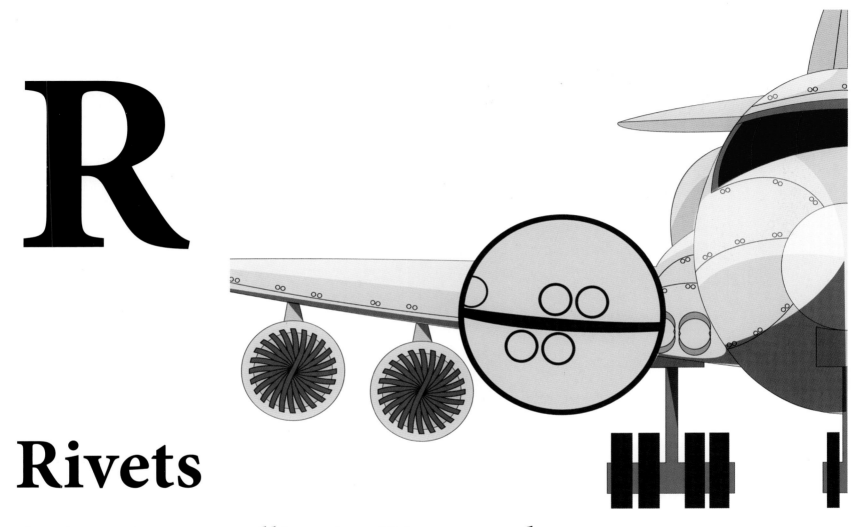

Rivets

A **rivet** is a metallic pin. Rivets make very strong, permanent connections. Do you know how many **rivets** are on an airplane?

S

Saw

A **saw** is a thin blade of metal with lots of small, sharp teeth. A **saw** is used for cutting things like wood or metal.

T

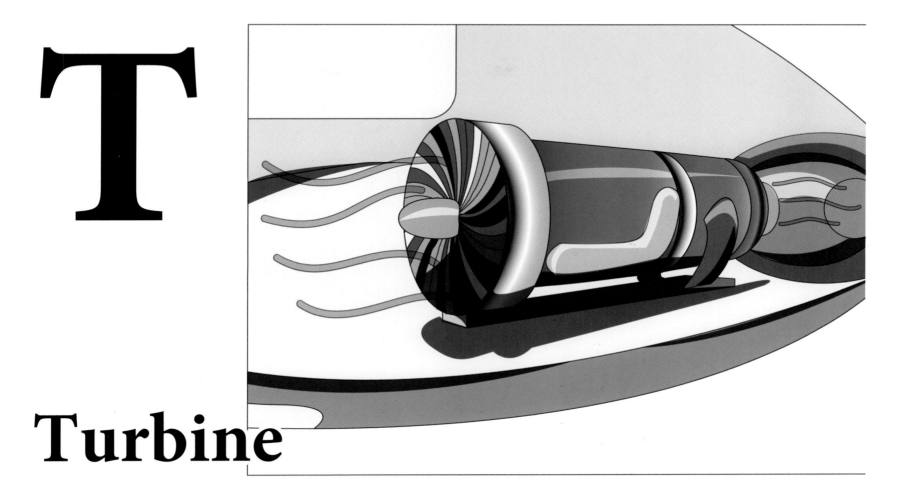

Turbine

A **turbine** is a type of engine that produces power. **Turbines** are used in jet planes, windmills, and dams.

U

Ultrasound

An **ultrasound** is a high frequency sound wave that humans cannot hear. Bats and dolphins communicate using **ultrasounds**.

Z

Zoetrope

A **zoetrope** is a device that gives the illusion of motion by a rotating drum moving through a series of still images.

Axle

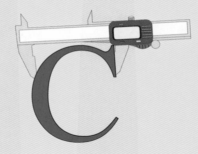

Beam

Caliper

Drill

Engine

Jigsaw

Kaleidoscope

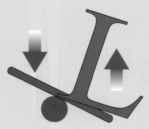

Lever

Mallet

Saw

Turbine

Ultrasound

Vise

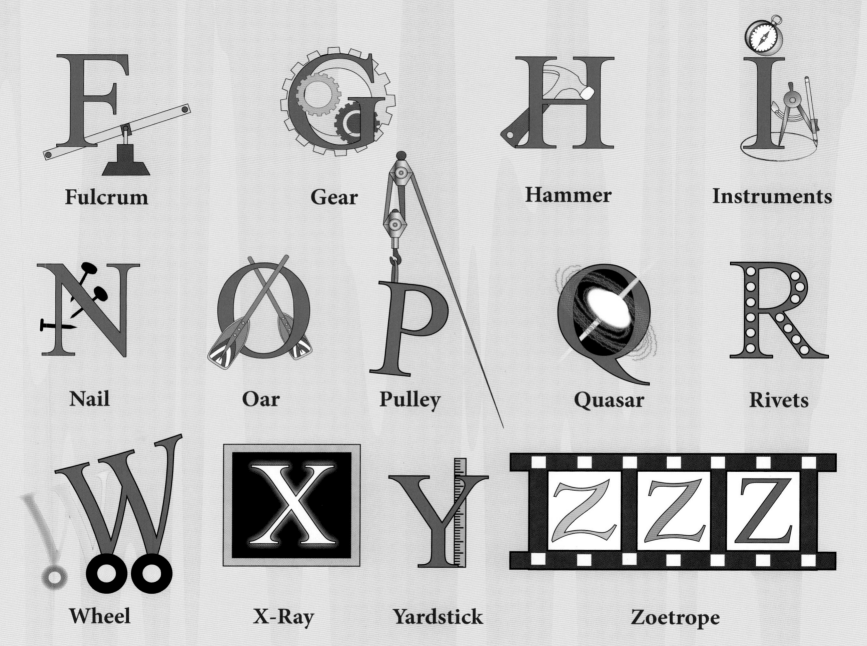

Fulcrum

Gear

Hammer

Instruments

Nail

Oar

Pulley

Quasar

Rivets

Wheel

X-Ray

Yardstick

Zoetrope

"TIME FOR TECH TERMS"

A axle, awl, ax	**B** beam, bushing, bolt				
C caliper, clamp, chisel	**D** drill, drawing, dongle	**E** engine, element, equipment	**F** fulcrum, force, funnel	**G** gear, gravity, gasket	**H** hammer, hinge, hacksaw
I instrument, i-beam, inertia	**J** jigsaw, jackhammer, joint	**K** kaleidoscope, knife, Kilogram	**L** lever, level, lathe	**M** mallet, mill, machine	**N** nail, nut, notch
O oar, odometer, o-ring	**P** pulley, pliers, pipe	**Q** quasar, quartz, quotient	**R** rivet, ruler, ratchet	**S** saw, screw, scissors	**T** turbine, tape, torque
U ultrasound, unit, upload	**V** vise, valve, vessel	**W** wheel, wrench, wire	**X** x-ray, x-axis, xylograph	**Y** y-axis, yoke, yardstick	**Z** zoetrope, zoom, zipper